JIG
TO
THE
JAZZ

by Carl M. Polaski
illustrations by Liisa Chauncy Guida

Harcourt Brace & Company

Orlando Atlanta Austin Boston San Francisco Chicago Dallas New York Toronto London

I can huff and puff.

I don't like to brag,

but I'm very gruff.

Here comes Pig.

I like pigs.

Pig has a wig!

The wig is as big

as Pig!

What is going on?

Look at Frog

tug the rug.

Look at Dog

drag the rug.

What is going on? 5

Pig does a jig!

Dog plays jazz!

Frog jumps zig-zag-zig!

I like to huff, puff,

and be gruff.

But . . .

I like to have fun, too!